Sundresses And Suits

By Dove Daniels

This book was semi-finished 5/30/2024-2:48 am

Aundrea Bloomington:

. . . It's the end of winter officially. I held onto my coat as long as I could.

  The day just kept getting hotter. I take a deep breath, shedding my clothes. It's too hot for jeans and everything else is at the dry-cleaners.

  My shoulders feel bare as the air hits them, a warmth surrounding me, pounding on my chest.

  I swallow harshly, glancing at the single dress hanging in my closet.

  It's discarded, brand-new. A bright sunny yellow with spaghetti straps. Arthur had bought it for me all too many years ago.

I feel around my jaw. A barely distinct slash where he had cut it open with a knife. Insane how a simple miscalculation of veggies could end in a fight.

I remember the blood gushing out like a water spout, sprinkling my white blouse.

I shudder despite the heat and slowly make my way to the dress, running my fingers down the hem of it.

The fabric is soft against my skin. Welcoming my stomach and flattering my hips and breasts.

I chew my lip, staring at myself in the mirror. There're bags under my eyes and scars all over me.

I trace a particularly thick one across my shoulder, thinking of how many men took advantage of me.

How many men *could* take advantage of me?

 Too many.

One is too many…

I swallow my doubts and spin, the bottom flares
out like a flower.

  I spare a smile, tiredly trailing my fingers through
my hair. I untie my pony tail and it falls just past
my elbows.

I learned to keep it up at the age of sixteen when
George Creeger and Alex Finnigan pinned me
against the tether ball wall and had their way with
me.

I gulped back the horrible memory of hair pulling, my torn navy-blue dress.

I shut my eyes before staring in the mirror again. "You've got this." I mumble to hype myself. I tie my running shoes and stand at the door. "It's worth it."

I tell myself before stepping out of the comfort of my own house.

The streets were noisy and colorful as I made my way to the library. Many cars rush by, honking horns and motorcycles. The glass doors shut behind me. I flinch at the loud noise. The building is quiet and almost completely empty of human life.

As always. Just how it should be. I walk up to the woman at the front desk, a redhead named Delilah.

"Good morning, Aundrea." She smiles at me in a non-threatening close-mouthed way. I nod to her and begin to slide down the aisles. I make my way to the learning section as I liked to call it. It was the aisle where all the books on '*how to*' were located. Also, self-help books.

My lips curve up as I trace the letters of them until finding one, I like the feel of. It's a rather large book on Tesla's. Not what I expected. I stroll down and to the right, to the back.

I am horrified to find that there is a person in my favorite seat. Not just a person. A *man*. He's sitting in my small beige chair at the white round table, large and taking up lots of space.

He looks intimidating, even just reading. Is he reading? He is. I notice a coffee cup next to his elbow.

My first reaction is to tell him off for bringing a beverage into the library. I'm almost to him before I think better of it.

I just stare, my mouth wide open. After a moment he lifts his head, turning and almost knocking over the cup. No matter how hard I try not to, we make eye-contact.

His are a gray-Ish deep, deep blue with the shape similar to an almond or a sideways tear-drop. He raises a bushy black eye-brawl.

"If you're wondering if you can check a person out you cannot."

His face splits into a wolf-like grin.

I feel my throat close up and I can't look away. I know I should be offended but all I can be is flustered. I lift my finger to argue but the words don't come out.

Suddenly the threatening grin switches to a close-lipped smile and he squints at me.

"I'm only kidding, god knows I can't flirt with a girl these days."

He sticks out his hand and I feel my ears pop. *Flirt with a girl? What's THAT supposed to mean?*

My feet drag themselves over the blue carpet and my hand is in his. He gives it one firm shake, once more making unwelcome and unwavering eye-contact.

"Frank, Frank White." I didn't ask. Who the hell is named *Frank White*? That's like the whitest guy name I've ever heard. I can't glare however. I just stare. His features are defined and symmetrical.

I don't tell him my name. Why should I? Why should I feel forced to give this stranger- His name is Frank white- information just because he forced his information?

"What are you reading?" I ask instead, still on-guard. It's your move and if I don't like it there's a knife in my bag and a pepper spray with *Frank White* on it, buddy. "Ah,"

He lets go of me and picks up a book from his table, page forty-two.

There's a book-mark that's actually an ad for two free dinners at an Italian restaurant. I stare at it in disbelief.

Is he seriously so stuck up his own that he's actually expecting me to go on a date with him? That's Assumptions' Aundrea. I remind myself, taking a deep breath.

“You're that Aundrea girl, correct?” “I see you here often.”

My eyes widened before narrowing. I was under the impression that I was alone.

 I shudder at the thought that he viewed every one of my smiles like something in the museum, heard every small laugh of mine and memorized it, tracked every aisle I moved through.

Oblivious. My fists clench and I wish I had pockets. Damn girl dress. Does he know where I *Live*? I feel my heart start to race.

 "You're in my seat." I finally say. "I'm aware, it's comfortable and it's not yours."

He winks, which could be perceived as playful and harmless but I scowl.

What an a-hole! I feel my skin tighten.

I feel *exposed*.

"There's a seat across from this one." He taps the table. I look over at the empty chair across from him.

Why don't you just go back to reading and stop expecting things from me?

He still just stares at me. Fine. I slump down into the chair and thump my book down. It's not that bad but his presence is not welcome and I want to make that known to him.

I open it harshly to the first page and still scowl at him. He just sits there and smiles.

What a jerk. Can't you see I'm uncomfortable? I noticed his attire. An Off-white coat with squares, white shirt, and white pants.

A watch that says he's got money to spend. I can't help but scowl all the more at his perfectly parted black and slick hair and his ruby-like lips. His mood is an obvious 'I'm important and I know it' way.

His Adams apple is noticeable, along with his jawline and the crevices of his collarbone. I swallowed back some saliva I hadn't realized had been accumulating in my mouth and finally looked away.

"Is that a book on cars?" He quirked at me, folding his hands.

"I didn't think you would be into that kind of thing." I blinked.

"What's that supposed to mean?" My words came out like venom. Vile in the back of my throat. Anger.

Something I could feel, control, hold onto and protect myself with. My anger was like a thick jacket.

I was almost grateful this man was so arrogant. He didn't seem surprised which made me even angrier. Who did he think he was?

"I like cars." I glared. It was nice to be able to glare. It wasn't necessarily a lie. Cars helped me get to different destinations and I felt safe in them.

"Hm." He looked back at his book and then began to *ignore* me. WHAT? I mumbled a curse and turned the page.

Most of the words I didn't really understand. I understood things such as breaks and steering but not things like tank and wrench.

What was a wrench? And why did they call the little ring things nuts? They didn't resemble any form of nut whatsoever.

Alright.

I'm not all that hard-headed. I'm willing to admit it's my fault and yes, it is my fault that I fall into the stereotype when I don't think to learn how a car works but- But nothing, Aundrea.

Just like that, the argument is over. I take a deep breath and glance up at his smirk.

I scoff. "Why so cocky?" "You're the one saying cocky, I'm simply smiling." He pointed to his admittedly cute dimple in the left corner of his cheek.

I blushed, digging my nails into my palms. For the rest of the two hours, I was there we sat and read separate books in silence.

I never did figure out what he was reading. He always covered the binding and once he stood, he held it under his arm.

I take a deep breath and glance up at him again. "Look, you're right but stop being so–" I realize he's gone. Up and left.

Well, I suppose that's why he grabbed his book but it was kind of rude.

I mentally kick myself for even fathoming the idea of enjoying his attention and missing it once he's already gone.

The rest of the day his smile played in my mind, his words swirling around my head. Each time like a horrid cheesy commercial I couldn't stop seeing the captions, singing the really bad lyrics to myself as I read or ate.

Even in the loo I sat there, thinking about him. Stupid guy. Stupid girl. I huffed and slammed my book down on my lap, only for it to fall on the bathroom floor.

It thudded loudly. This gained a few women's attention and I winced. Stupid, *stupid* girl.

The following day I practically ran across the street. Luckily traffic wasn't as unexplainably horrendous as usual.

Either that or I tuned it out. I swear I was walking on clouds, dancing on lavender and humming a sweet melody with my hair down once more in a little orange sundress.

The dress barely passed my knees and it had oranges on it. I actually wore jewelry.

Getting in touch with my feminine side as the ladies of the internet would say. I felt a little ridiculous, sliding down the halls of the library.

My destination? A very up his own guy with stunning eyes.

There he was. Sitting in my chair. I glowered at him, my heart fluttering.

What was happening? I wasn't doing all this for him. I was definitely doing it for me.

As a woman in make-up would do. I took a deep breath, willing my breath to even out.

Willing my heart to stop the joyous skipping. *We're not doing this again.* I scolded. I plopped down in front of him and he glanced up from his book with an amused glint.

"Good morning, Aundrea." I nodded, trying to be nonchalant.

I set my bag down by the leg of my *new* chair and stared at the library from this perspective. I only ever stared at the wall.

Now I could see all the aisles, symmetrical like his face, lined up in columns with multi-colored and shaped books.

I almost smiled at the sight. He caught my lip twitch and grinned like that wolf I knew all too well. "Are you tired?" I blinked. "Well-"

"Because you've been running through my mind all night." I rolled my eyes, slapping open my book to a random page.

Photos of different car parts foreign to me.

"Cheezy and pathetic." I muttered. However, all I could do was think 'Same'. He shrugged, all laxed and chill, turning the page.

"What are you reading?" I asked again.

He didn't respond. I attempted to lean over and peak but he covered most of it with his big gray-suited arm.

I made a dramatic wine and to my surprise he laughed. I felt a tad bit of pride at that. I made him laugh.

Hah! My heart leaped in victory and I chastised it again. It refused to stop cartwheeling. Apparently, my heart must have been chasing an Olympic record.

"You brought coffee *again*?" I observe. He grabs his cup, smirking. Jerk. "Yep, want some?" "From the same cup!" I stare at him, aghast.

"Yes, is that so *crazy* to you?" He teases. I grip the cup and snatch it from his hand. To my horror it spills a little.

"Mrs. Bloomington." A hoarse voice whispers.

I gulp, being reminded of the Harry-Potter Audio book, when He Who Must Not Be Named is speaking in parseltongue.

Frank's eyes are blown wide and his face is pale, his lips thin with remorse. "That is two warnings do not have another."

And with that, the She Who Must Not Be Named Librarian's assistant is gone, her auburn perm shook aggressively at me as she walked away.

I take a large gulp of it and realize it's *very* hot. I finish it off anyway, letting out a smokey breath that I'm positive I saw a glimpse of fire in.

The look of second-hand embarrassment and almost apology is replaced by that stupid smirk again, making my face turn redder somehow.

"I have a sandwich as well if you would like another warning." I slap his hand away and he holds them up in surrender, grinning. Stupid *handsome* guy.

Stupid girl.

"I'm famished." He clearly didn't expect me to take him up on the offer but if he wants to play that game two can play.

"Alright, well *I* have a record free library card and I'd like to keep it that way so come on."

I look at him, accusingly as he stands up, book clasped under his arm, yet again unreadable.

"Where are you going?" "The exit is that way." I point to the front but he shakes his head, running a hand through his jet-black hair.

I'm momentarily hypnotized by it before I remember I'm not some stupid blonde swooned female who can't help herself but fall for Mr. *Smith*. I mean come on.

Despite my better self I follow him to what seems to be the back left side of the library.

Never been there. Didn't ever need to. "This is also an exit."

I blink at the obvious door his hand is on. I nod and he pushes it open, revealing *a whole new world*.

It's a little brisk outside but nothing I can't handle. The leaves are a vibrant green, on the floor and in clumps on trees.

Bright blue and orange and gray birds tweeted happily, dancing in their nests, nuzzling above fresh batches of eggs.

I was mesmerized for lack of a better word. He guided me up three grassy hills with tiny colorful flowers to a wooden bench.

Four tall red-oaks loomed over it, creating some sort of beautiful archway that both shaded and lit the magical spot.

I felt the breeze in my hair as we sat down, thigh to thigh on the bench. I trusted that my bag would be safe back in the library.

I accidentally left it by my seat, blindly following Frank. I couldn't believe I had let my fear of exploring more of the library hold me back from this little slice of paradise.

I opened my book on my lap and crossed my legs. I didn't care what the internet said for just a moment. *Be vulnerable.* A sweet little voice whispered in my head.

I leaned on his broad shoulder as we silently read about odd car parts and what they're uses were, how to change the oil, how frequently, and why gas cars were a thing. It actually started to make sense. Was Instagram wrong? I blinked the thought away, pushing off of Frank.

 What was I doing? He grabbed my wrist, gently and stared at me with a smile. "I know another great place if you'll trust me, Aundrea."

"This is the spot?" I blinked, horrified. I thought he meant a private pool. Not a *public* water park. I held my white robe tight against my chest.

I hadn't realized there would be kids here. "Who are they?" I whispered. "My mother, my aunt, my cousins and strangers."

 He gave me that wolf-Ish grin then he disrobed and I had to do a double take. How could he be so slick and careful yet so beasty?

 I was disgusted at my own vulgar mind and begged myself to stop monologuing how perfect his abs were.

He was shirtless with black swimming trunks with thick lines. "Stop..." I muttered, commanding myself. Finally, I let up, letting fear consume me. There were so very many people there.

All from least threatening to absolutely horrible. I squeeze the braided belt of my only coverage and brace it like a shield against the world.

Me vs everything.

"Come on, stop being such a baby I'm sure you look great Aundrea."

I shut my eyes and shed my protection. There's silence. I open them and he's just staring at me, thin lips and all. Um hello? "Wow."

Is all he says. Wow, really? "What's that supposed to mean?" "Uh, come on, let's get in the pool!" He grips my wrist with his strong hand.

I am lifted off one leg and dragged across the pavement. I can walk by myself.

The cement path was hot on my feet and I was relieved to suddenly be up to mid-hip in clear unreal blue water.

It makes my legs look odd. I've been to a pool before, of course, but it's been a long time.

"You do look really nice." He whispers in my ear, tucking some of my hair behind it. I gulp, feeling numb. I didn't like that my friend could do this to me.

He was a friend. Right. *Just a particularly attractive male friend.* I pulled away and sat down. The water rose to my shoulders.

"You're going to stay there?" He asks, now laying in the water, holding himself up on his fingertips

I don't know how he does it.

Why were you so eager to see what he thought of how you look? You know better than that. I shudder.

"Aren't you going to go deeper?" He chuckles, making my cheeks burn.

"Are you?" I retorted. He smirks, raising one of those stupid bushy brawls. "Only if you want me to, Aundrea." With that he kicks off, splashing me. "I..." "Hey!"

"You arrogant donkey!" I swim farther into the deep end, feeling my carefree strokes coming back to me now.

I kick and paddle and turn and grasp his muscular calf. He laughs and stays put, grinning at me.

It's threatening. Right? He laughs. "Tag!" A much smaller hand touches my shoulder.

What the hell? It's a kid who doesn't yet know the danger of a stranger. He giggles and paddles off. "What do I do?" I stare at Frank for help.

 "Tag me." He smirks, a playful glint in those deep blue eyes. I listen to the man for once in a very long time and tap his chest. It's a hard pec.

Damn. He grins wolf-like and dashes off deeper into the big pool.

There's more squealing giggling and a little girl, she giggles, a little boy, another girl and finally a little hand on my shoulder.

"Wait a minute!" I laugh, giving into the craziness for just a *moment* and exploring more of the pool.

With wet bare-feet I climb up a web like thing which leads to a bigger platform in the middle of the pool.

I'm surprised it's holding my weight as I stupidly slide down a small yellow tube.

It fits and goofy child faces stare at me through clear circles in it. I come out the other end, almost sliding out the spout.

I hop back into the water, hiding low like a shark. A pale tiny leg.

"Gotcha!" It's a little girl with long soaked black hair.

She screams, giggles and chases after more children. I've never laughed so much I think in my life.

I missed this. I missed when the world was safe for little girls and little boys. I gulped down the thought with a slug of bubbly Pepsi.

In a *red plastic cup*. I wasn't doing much for saving the environment but I was finally living a little, almost edging out of my shell.

I like my shell. It could get a little lonely though.

Lonely? Since when was *that* in our vocabulary? "Tag!" I'm hit again and I paddle after a little redheaded boy, kicking his feet. Ewe! Feet water! I groan and tag him.

He squeaks, rushing down the second tallest slide. Sometimes I felt like a water park in winter.

Empty, un-lively, mourning the loss of children and adults in my life. I used to dream of having kids, with Author but I never really thought of them again.

Now I was thinking of them. No matter how badly I didn't want to, I kept picturing them, dark blonde hair or even black with *his* (Blue) eyes and my nose, his grin a little boy and a little girl.

My heart felt heavy and I sank into the cold water, thanking I'm not sure who just someone, out there potentially having done this for me. Perhaps the guy who maintained the pool.

I rushed back up, gasping, my hair soaked, running down my shoulders and breasts.

"Hey," I opened my eyes to see Frank. He was grinning as I imagined my son definitely not *our* son doing so. "Hey yourself." I gasped out, squeezing a lock of my hair.

"Wasn't that fun?" "I got you a watermelon popsicle." "How'd you know I like watermelon?" "Lucky guess."

I take it hesitantly and give it a lick. He watches me intensely.

I close my eyes once more and continue to enjoy the cool fresh fruity flavors on my tongue.

I grunt and hum involuntarily as I finish it off.

His pupils are widened to where his blue eyes look almost black but he seems to remember this is a family friendly park, smiling and grabbing me yet again.

 This time I don't protest, letting myself be dragged.

 He brings me to dry land and we sit on warm blue and pink towels. "Wow you got me a *pink* towel."

 I attempt to be offended but I'm too giddy to put too much thought into it, lying back on the white plastic pull-out.

"Aw, I forgot to put sun-screen on!" I pop open my eyes to see that we did. Our skin makes us look like lobsters with blonde and black hair.

I groan and he laughs, hardily from the bottom of his belly. I rub some on my forearms and face. "Can you get my back?" He asks.

 I'm about to protest but he looks so innocent and helpless, reaching around but never quite touching. I know that itch all too well.

Let go of yourself. "Sure." I scoot on my knees and he sits on half my towel, handing me the plastic orange and white bottle.

 It's only now that I'm running my moist hands down his back that I *really* feel the waves, bumps, crevices and contours of his body.

I blush deeply and attempt to stomp it. Not that he can see. That thought is a little relaxing as I dip down, rubbing it over the last bit of his lobster back.

"Here I'll do yours." "Unless..." He goes on, staring at my pink face and parted lips.

"You'd rather be boiled and cracked open, dipped in ranch?" I blink. Why was that so sensual? Maybe I'm just hungry.

"Really?" But the joke was pretty cute. He does an adorable- Uh oh. Adorable? -

Shrug. At the same time, we speak up again as his warm hands meet my skin, only slightly cold from the cream. "I don't know about you but I kind of want sea-food now."

We laugh in union and the rest is silent. He finished up, his cheeks tinted pink as well. Victory. Victory? Let me have this one.

 I don't know how 'Sea-food' turned into '*Italian date' but here we were.* Me curling my messy hair and battling my chipped, dry and sentries' old eye-liner.

 My make up kit looks back at me sadly like I abandoned it.

 I didn't abandon it par-say. I just didn't feel the need or want to put on face paint and powder after Arther.

The restaurant is expensive. I can tell. How am I going to afford this? He doesn't seem bothered however.

He glances over the big plastic menu and I can't help but think how stereotypical this is. Here I am in a stupid forest green dress, complimenting my figure that *he* bought.

Why am I here?

Why am I wearing this?

With *him*?

What am I doing?

I feel dizzy as I stare at him. The picture of calm, laid back even with his legs spread wide and planted on the floor like a strong tree with his nice suit and fancy dumb pocket square.

I'm drawn to the crease between his eye-brawls, the exposed neck, his gruff hands and...

Those lips. I fiddle with my fingers under the table. Why am I staring at a man's lips?

What are my eyes doing? I pray I'm not giving him 'f-ck me' eyes. I take a sip of my water, the ice cubes clinking the edges of the glass. It burns my teeth in the way that only cold can.

"What would you like to order, Aundrea?" I didn't prepare for that.

What's English again? Instead, I mumble something incoherent and shyly smile, staring at my toes sticking out of my white toeless heels.

I never thought I'd be wearing something like this again but here I was. Why did I *want* to dress up for this man? I knew I shouldn't. Right? "Are you alright?"

He's asking me more questions and I curse him in my head for his stupid concerned handsome face. Handsome? Am I turning red?

It's really stuffy here. I stand up. The fancy white chair scrapes across the floor and I'm dashing. Dashing as fast as I can in these heels.

I slam open the women's bathroom door and slam my hand on the blue marbled counter.

"Why did I say handsome?" I whisper to myself, taking off my shoes. My pinkie toes are red. I rub them in circles. "I don't know."

 A deep voice I don't recognize. I feel my heart beat quicker as an unwelcome hand, sets itself in my hair with a firm fat fingered grip.

Please.

"You look nice in that." *Please*. It's a man I mean... I don't know they're in a dress and tights but he's grabbing me and I don't like it.

 "Sir please let go of me." I calmly speak. "It's ma'am." The gruff voice responds. I gulp. He's not letting go.

I feel a tear running down my cheek. "M-Ma'am please let me go." "I'm uncomfortable." I feel so small.

Another tear and my mascara is thick, slopping and sticking my eye-lashes together. Why did I ever put on makeup again, again?

"You're fine." They grunt, pressing themselves against my back.

They're much taller than me, one hand in my hair the other pushing down on my shoulder. "Please," I whimper.

I can't seem to get a break. I knew this was a bad idea. All of this. Him, the dinner, the not-flirting everything.

It all flashes in front of me, his eyes, his threatening slash non-threatening smile, his chuckle that makes my throat swell.

"*Frank*," I whisper. The person tugs on my hair and it burns as I fight to pull away.

More grayish tears gush down my neck, staining the hemming of my new dress.

I'm running out of the bathroom, that man is left with some blond hair and my shoes. I'm faster without them.

I'm not running towards the door and down the side-walk and I'm not grabbing my purse.

I'm burrowing in a solid warm chest; steady breathing and strong arms enclose me.

I sob and shiver.

   He whispers things I cannot understand in my ears until he tells me to stay put.

   He pushes me down in a non-painful way into his seat and I feel weak. Too weak to fight, I just sit there with my eyes shut tightly, probably glued together by thick moist make-up caked onto my face.

   I sort of forgot how to apply it after all these years.

Chapter eleven: Cherry Seven-up

I hold the cloth covering me. It's warm and it's there. It comforts me as I tilt my sorry head down, my head pulsing from where they had ripped my hair. It feels like only a few seconds before Frank is back.

His eye-brows are furrowed and he's wiping his fist with a napkin.

He moves towards me and for once I don't flinch. I let him touch my face, examine my lips and finally give a nod.

He grabs my arms and pulls me out of the chair, holding me close to his side.

I say nothing as he slaps a fifty on the table, stuffing his wallet back into his pocket. I feel his big warm hand on my thigh through his jacket and it doesn't feel scary.

He walks me to his car and buckles me in like a child. I don't fight it, still silently sniffling. Everything is working *against* me and this *change* except *him*.

I'm absorbed in that smell of books and cologne with leather and mint.

The smell of utter masculinity and old yet beautiful paper.

It's not overwhelming this time. I smell it deeply, relaxing into it and letting myself sink, letting my tired head fall back.

I wake up without screaming. I don't recognize this place.

The lights are dim and I'm sitting on a couch, a big flat screen in front of me, a glass coffee table and white carpet.

The temperature is warm. His coat is still on me and I'm still in my soaked dress.

He didn't change me. He respected my privacy?

I realize it's *his house*.

I snap my head to the noise. It's Frank. He walks into the room with a glass bowl of popcorn. Popcorn? On his other hand are two crossed and somehow balanced wine glasses.

"Frank?" My throat hurts as my voice cracks. "What's with the wine?" I tuck my knee's in. He was waiting till I was awake and now he's going to make me drink and force me.

I curl even more. "Pft, wine?" He laughs, setting down his stuff and pushing the table towards me. He sits beside me, bringing me to his hip.
It's not uncomfortable.

I glare at the mysterious beverage, as it bubbles, accusing it.

"Yea." "Right." It pops and bubbles and I stare. "You want a silly straw?"

He blinks, a stupid smile playing on his lips. I scowl.

"For wine?" "It's not alcoholic!" He insists, laughing at me. Rude. "Alright, then what is it?" I huff.

"This is Cherry seven-up."

He pops a lime green swirl straw into the wine glass and takes a drink, making eye-contact. Why is that hot? I question my mental health.

Who am I kidding? I've always questioned it.

"If you don't want any then fine."
He reaches his hand into the popcorn bowl and throws some into his mouth. It smacks him in the eye-lid but he eats it anyway.

What is happening?

Is this *cute*?

Deciding it's harmless I take *his* glass and sip. It bubbles and pops and it's not wine. It's cherry seven-up and it's delicious.

"I got you a glass." He glares but it's playful. I shrug, relaxing a little and I even smirk.

"Ow- Ow oh crap," He grunts. I laugh and reach in taking a scoop of flavor.

"Hold on, I've got to rinse out my eyes before I start crying in front of a girl."

"Oh gosh forbid you show weakness."

I roll my eyes as he gets up and I can't say that I didn't watch his fine ass as he leaned over the sink.

He comes back, hair and face wet. The top of his shirt soaked too.

He grins, flashing his straight white teeth. "Stop being hot." "What?" Oh *crap*.

"I said that out loud?" He just laughs and pats my leg.

"Calm down, I know I'm sexy." "Not sexy, I said hot." I protest, dipping into the popcorn again.

It's good too. A completely different burst of spice from what I just tasted.

It's peppery and cheesy and buttery. "Do you like it?" He changes the subject. I'm grateful. "I love it."

Woah. Love? A little strong for popcorn talk.

"Nice, it's cheddar with orange Cheeto and hot Cheeto dust, cyan, chili, a squirt of sriracha and tabasco."

I gulp as my throat begins to burn and my eyes tear again. This time I'm laughing, giggling even. "Well, it's really good." He smiles.

Is that blush on his cheeks and up his neck from the popcorn or me?

Why do you care?

Why are you still staring at his neck?

Okay recap. He gets you to be more feminine, he takes you on fancy dates, he defends you, he likes books spice and crazy flavors, he dresses like a businessman and he's respecting and not respecting my boundaries.

He has to be a serial killer. He just has to be. I glare at him, stuffing more popcorn into my mouth.

The cyan makes my lips sting.
He's juggling his, missing his mouth almost every single time and he's laughing, crow's feet, dimples and all.

Am I in love?

I ignore the thought as it makes a loud bright red siren go off in my head and I'm enjoying my moment. My moment?

I ignore that too, shutting down my defenses just this once as this stupid dream man continues to throw the popcorn around.

I wake up and run a hand through my hair. It's tangled. Damn. What time is it? The bed is warm. I roll over to see a black digital clock with red blinking numbers.

I sit up and rub my eyes. My makeup is gone?

I don't remember washing it off. It's just barely twelve in the afternoon. The bed is empty.

It's not my bed. I blink, surveying the room. Holy crap. What happened? I remember popcorn and smiles and spice, my lips tingling.

Did we? No... He couldn't have...

My legs didn't give out from pain as I stood. I stood perfectly fine.

There's a mirror by the door. Should I snoop? I decided against it.

"I do have to pee." I mumble, my voice groggy. I begin the journey down the hall.

After feeling around the room, I find another door. It's the bathroom. *His* bathroom.

I give myself brownie points and push open the door. It smells just like him. I sit down on the toilet and almost fall in.

"Crap!" I yipe, setting the toilet rem down.

Finally, Peaceful. Until I fall in, butt first. Something comes to mind.

#LiveLifeButtFirst.

I laugh loudly, coiling as clean but cold toilet water sloshes around me.

I think some went in my butthole. Ew!

I push my way out and drop the second section of the toilet very loudly.

"Frank, would you please close the toilet next time?" Next time? "Ah,"

He drops something behind the counter and bends down to pick it up.

"Shoot, sorry yeah I'll remember that next time." Next time? "I believe." He mumbled as I sat down at the counter.

"I just messed up the eggs."

 A laugh tears from my throat. "Sorry." I mutter, stifling it with my hand.

 He looks at the mess of eggs in the metal dust pan with such sad-eyed disappointment. It reminded me of a puppy. I pat his back.

 He calms down, slumping his shoulders and tipping the screwed-six-ways-from-Sunday eggs into the metal tin.

 Why did it feel good to calm him? Why did I need to comfort him? Why did I *want* to comfort this *man*? I retract my hand and sit back down.

I watch as he cracks two more eggs into a pan, looking more determined than ever. I smile for some reason I can't bother to comprehend.

Live this moment in bliss and suffer later.

I tell myself. He finally sets a plate with an omelet on it in front of me, looking smug.

I roll my eyes and stab a fork into the corner.

"Taste like; cheesy egg." He stares at me, frowning slightly. I notice his ear-piece isn't in. It's nice. Just us.

No possible agents or gosh forbid-..girlfriend listening. *Girlfriend?*

His house just looks empty if anything.

"Take a bigger bite, get some of that bacon and tomato in there!" He insisted. I do as told, grimacing at the thought of grilled tomato.

 I chew. It pops. A blast of salty and savory flavors. It's amazing. I never thought I would ask an omelet to marry me but maybe this was the right omelet.

 The right omelet? Getting a little comfortable are we Aundrea? I swallow and choose to keep eating it. Scarfing and swallowing the fluffy eggs.

 I don't dare look at his smirking face. He sits across from me at the counter instead of the table and all that could be heard is clinking scraping and chewing.

 "Huh." "Not my best." He declares. I scoff, tempted to lick the bacon grease from my plate.

My mind chooses to replay him shirtless in his swimming trunks followed by his grin and him throwing popcorn into his mouth.

Goon.

"Not your best?" I argue. "Meh, give or take a seven and a half I can do better." He looks so settled with himself.

"I demand it's better than that."

There's a glint in his deep blue eyes that makes me question if we're still talking about omelets and then it's gone.

He smiles, stands up and sets the dishes in the sink. I feel tempted to do them.

Why?

Why should I do his dishes? I'm not his maid. Was it because he cooked and welcomed me into his home with kindness or was it because I am brainwashed into thinking that's what females do?

"Frank, where's my purse?" "On the sofa where you left it, honey."

He says it in a silly voice from his bedroom but I grow flustered, my hands sweaty and something in my loins clenching and aching.

The hell? Why is it doing that?

Not now!

I reach into the tan tote-bag before pulling my hand back out. I'm *deciding* to help a *male friend* out.

After a few minutes I dry my hands and Franks walks down the hall.

I dropped my phone before I could even unlock it.

What the sh–? His short black hair is slick back, in a bob- style, his ear piece in yet again, tight, tight black pants and Italian leather shoes a black blazer and a red tie matching pocket square.

"What is that for?" I breathe, squeezing my hands together so tight it burned the sides of my fingers. Gentle unwelcome water droplets beaded down his hair and his eyebrows, collecting at the bottom of his collarbone.

I chewed my tongue. "My job." He blinked at me, acting like he didn't know how hot he looked. I was swooning.

WHY was I swooning?

I gulp. He flicks his hair with two fingers and taps his neck, smiling. Hot. Stop. Seriously.

"You're welcome to stay as long as you'd like, honey." He winks at me, then he leaves. Aw. My reply. Now I'm alone in a stranger.

Frank's house. It's big, it's gorgeous and it's *empty*. I wonder what his job is as I run my fingers over the wall. I should feel unsafe but I don't. I feel warm and cozy.

Even *welcome*.

I feel a strike of panic followed by dopamine and I do a childish thing. I get up and dance.

I don't know what time I ended up heading home. I remember falling asleep and then leather and books followed by waking up in my own bed.

I yawn and tuck my hair behind my ears.

I decided to get up early, take a shower and yes, I bought another sundress because he loves it when I wear them.

It's blue with white floral print and puffy shoulders.

It flows just past my knees in two sections, fit together with a big bow at the back. I even curled my hair. I felt so giddy to see him, getting to *our* table early.

I don't see him. I don't see him for hours. I lean on the table, read through books and he's still not there.

My smile is gone.
I'm no longer giddy or flushed. He stood me up.
After I actually went on a stupid stereotypical date and even *slept* beside him.

My stomach twists again as I begin to think we did have sex last night. I tuck my tail between my legs and head home.

I'm now in a baggy t-shirt and shorts. I haven't worn these in a while. I turned on my phone for the first time.

Something about voting season being over and... Huh?

I ignore everything else because there's an unknown number.

[Busy day at work, a lot of people showed up.]

[It's Frank.]

Proper grammar and lack of this gen lingo is a little scary. I read on.

[How are you?]

[I wish I could read with you.]

[Wish I had popcorn.]

[You should try my chili.]

[Check out this badge.]

A picture attached.

I yawn, my eyes watery and click on it. It's a box image of his deep blue suit, his red pocket square and a sparkling pride pen. I read the thick shining letters.

Pride-so-dent. What?

[Ridiculous right?]

[Who are they to assume I'm queer let alone support the alphabet club?]

I laugh.

The alphabet club. We can crack jokes at them like everything else. Right? "Okay Mr. president." I mock allowed. How arrogant the goofball.

He sent a meme of a two-sided photo.
A monkey in an animated suit hovering over a banana and keys.

 The other photo was a man in a real suit, hovering over unreadable documents.

The captions on both ends were 'Making tough decisions and cuts.'

I laughed again, covering my mouth despite being alone in my own house.

 [Today was stressful but I look forward to seeing your face.]

With a wink emoji and a photo attached to it. I blushed and clicked on it a little too quickly.

It was a photo of him lying back in his bed, the bed I recognized, his head resting on a pillow, a hand carefree through his black hair.

He was wearing a gray shirt. It was only the top of him but his smile suggested something that made my head spin.

I blushed harder, grinning like a schoolgirl and screenshotted it.

[Goodnight.]

Was the last thing he sent.
I shut off my phone and plugged it in on my dresser, biting my lip and shutting my eyes.

That image would live *rent free* in my head.

[I can't leave the office today; my adviser says little library dates with a cute girl are pointless.]

[I beg to differ.]

[My cute girl means the world to me.]

I blushed. Yeah, I technically got stood up again but it wasn't his fault, right?

  I sat here in another green sundress at our table. I wasn't supposed to really have my phone in the library but I just couldn't help it.

[My?] He doesn't spare me a second.

  [Yup.]

[What's that supposed to mean?]

I feel myself smiling as he pops up with another response.

[Why do you want to know so bad, Aundrea?]

I shiver and run a hand through my hair. "No phones in the library."

 Oh sh-t. I grunt and quickly slam my thumb on the keypad.

[Gtg librarian says no phone lol love you... I stare at the unsent text and delete everything.

 [I have to go bye]

Ominous but there's no changing it now.

Chapter sixteen: Meeting with the Queen? As if.

I push open the backdoor of the building and there it is, the little bench in the center of four tall trees.

I settle down, remembering the feeling of Frank's thigh flush against mine as we read side-by-side. I blush.

A ghost ache and shiver creep up my neck and my legs feel staticky.

I open my phone again, glaring at it with my hand shading my eyes from the bright sun.

[Alright, I have a meeting with the new queen to attend as well.]

I wait for hours, trying to understand the car book, kicking my legs back and forth and having a little nap.

Finally, my phone vibrates just slightly and I swipe up.

[Meet me--]

I click on the link before I finish reading and then find that it's next Tuesday I'm supposed to meet him.

My heart slows down.

[How was the meeting with 'The Queen'?]

I roll my eyes, grinning from ear-to-ear.

[Bland.] One word. Yikes. Whoever he was meeting didn't live up to his expectations. I smiled wider at this.

I definitely wasn't jealous at the thought of another woman monopolizing my *male friend*'s time.

"At last, a moment peace, right?" I smile at Frank. We're in a small coffee shop just off the side of the city.

"Yes, it's nice to not have to deal with work and to be able to hang out with Aundrea, the super rad cute girl who wears sundresses for me."

"Why so secluded?" I ask, glancing around the empty tables. "To hide." He smiles and the thought of a secret girlfriend comes to mind.

He places his larger hand over mine and makes eye-contact. "Fans and followers." I laugh. *Oh.* He's so stuck up his own but all his other attributes make up for it.

Making excuses for him, are we?

I shake my head and smile, relieved for the moment.

"Rad?" "Am I rad now?" He nods, taking a drink of his coffee. His gulps, looking like he's trying so hard to not be repulsed.

"Can't handle black coffee?" I grin, tapping the table. "Of course I can." He winces, taking another drink and swallowing.

"I'm a big strong man, I can take it." He insists, smirking. "Oh, can you now?" "Besides, I need the caffeine." He mutters and I notice the bags under his eyes.

Now where did those come from? There's a crease in his forehead that is a tall tale. He's exhausted. What's making him so exhausted?

I'm stopped by a donut being shoved into my mouth.

He's grinning, smushing the whole thing in.

I blush and try my best to chew. He looks so satisfied yet tired. Why is he tired?

"It's mango strawberry cream-filled; only this cafe has such crazy flavors." He smiles.

I nod. "It's pretty good but it's no- spicy cheesy popcorn."

"Or cherry seven-up." If there had been anyone around us they wouldn't understand a Knick of our personal jabs and flirting but I was floating, giddily blushing with quick personal replies.

It felt like it was *just us* which was accurate because well it was *just us*.

I smiled at this, letting myself give in and hold his bigger soft hand.

No ring.

How had I not checked for a ring before?

I felt a wave of relief wash over me. No girls to gawk at him, no ring, no worries.

Many worries! The other half of my mind wheezed and screamed but I ignored it.

Let me be that *stupid girl* for just a little while.

He grinned back at me, all lovesick like then his eyes widened and his lips tightened.

Dimple gone. Happiness?

Gone.

What did I do? I was about to ask what was wrong when he grabbed my arm, not in a painful way but I definitely knew to shut my mouth.

What was going on? I caught a flash and then another flash before he dragged me behind the little cafe. "Our donuts!"

I protested, out of breath for having walked or been dragged blocks down.

His face was pale again and a crease between his brawls told me that there was something to worry about.

"You're not telling me anything!"

 I shouted. "Please!" "Is it a wife?" I sounded so pitiful, pounding on his chest but he stayed silent, just staring at me.

 Finally, I curled into his chest.

"It's not a wife, honey you know that."

 "I thought you knew that I—" Suddenly a black limousine pulls up and a fancy arm snatches the sleeve of Frank.

He's yanked into it and I shout but the car drives off. All I catch is "Mr. Pr——-- what– are y--u d——--ou- here!" Who was that?

Did Frank just get kidnapped?

All I know now is that I'm obviously alone, in this stupid thin brown sundress, with a starving passion and I'm miles from anywhere.

And then it starts to drip. IN SUMMER.

And then it starts to pour. *In summer.*

No texts, no calls, no explanations. I've tried to report him missing but everyone just laughs in my face and tells me the same thing.

 'I'd think we would know if *Frank White* were kidnapped' 'Hardy Har-harr.'

 I groan into my tear-soaked pillow. I haven't left the house in weeks.

 I haven't been online at all either. It will just depress me and tell me how wrong and racist and homophobic I am.

 "Well, I'm *sorry* for *living*." I growl bitterly. I sob again, clutching my bed sheets tightly.
 I always thought he would text and tell me sorry or I would get a distressed call from him saying that he had little time but *here's my location*.

Nothing.

 I slope down-stairs and finally turn on the Tv. I click through a few shows before I land on the news.

"Yes, tell me about the weather." I whisper, hysterically. How could I *possibly* let another stupid up his own man make me feel this way again?

Hurt me like this-

-AGAIN?
I sniffle, wiping my nose with my finger. My pitiful train of thought slams into a brick wall as an image appears on screen.

I cannot believe my puffy red eyes or my buzzing ears. This has to be some big prank.

  Multiple photos of Frank and I including our private text messages are on screen but that's not even the thing that makes my stomach drop.

  It's that they're under thick black letters of a local news-story copied over onto an Instagram post. 'Hello, hello, Mr. White and Mrs. White?'

  Blinking unacceptable unbelievable UNTRUE it's got to be. Words swish over slide after slide with hashtags and all.

"Recently elected Frank White, has got a girlfriend?

Where is she now?

Aundrea? Last name unknown.

Mr. White's into nerdy chicks?

Why this loner?

Who is she?

Coffee dates, flirty photos and homophobic comments found on *Not so perfect* president's private account.

'Why her?' Begs a beautiful Latina woman one Sunday evening. Multiple ladies and men agree.

Filthy cheater! A mob cries and chants."

Even worse are photos of Frank.

My Frank with a man? A handsome blonde man with puppy dog eyes and a smile that tugs on heartstrings.

Girlfriend?

Gay?

Loner?

I'm not THAT lonely.

Am I?

Who's this guy?

Apparently, my life is a lie because for the past six months I've been dating the *president*.

My stomach bottoms out at live footage of Frank standing tall in front of thousands of people, staying absolutely silent and waving his hand to dismiss them all.

The first thing I do, after sobbing and questioning my life decisions *yet again* and scolding myself for believing in another man, I call Frank.

"Meet me at our spot."

"The only one where there aren't thousands of photos online of..." Heavy breathing and muffled shouting in the background.

I watch his live reaction, a stone expression, phone to his ear and tapping his foot against the podium.

He doesn't say a thing and I continue. "Or... this little whatever you call it thing going on between us..." "-Is over."

I whisper, tearily, hanging up. I drop my phone onto the sofa, feeling more tears gush down.

His eyes visibly widen and he drops his phone. A sea of people scrambles to take it, dissect it but he looks as if he couldn't care less.

He looks paler than I've ever seen him.

I un-mute the Tv. "Mr. President, Mr. President!" A distressed voice shrieks as he practically jumps into doom, running through the crowd that screams and shouts as they claw at him.

I Finally leave my apartment and speed-walk down the street to the *library*.

I leave my phone.

Why would I need it?

I stare up at the leaves of the trees. It's awfully hot today as the sun blares down through the cracks. The spot still feels beautiful and magical.

I still feel the ghost touch of Frank's leg up against mine, my cheek on his shoulder. A single tear drips down my chin. Footsteps. I look up.

Mr. President is white as a sheet. "I'm so sorry-" He begins, I stare at him. "I never wanted to involve you in this.

I tried my hardest to hide you from them, we both know what this risks and I... I thought maybe... But I wanted so desperately to call or even text!" "They took my phone!"

He's waving his arms and hunching over, panting. I scowl at him with puffy eyes. "What about the fact that your- Mr. President!" I shout at him, standing up.

He looks at me with confusion and I'm livid. "You- What?" He blinks at me with that stupid handsome repulsive face.

My heart raps and bangs on my lungs and my ribcage, fighting to get out. How could I be so *stupid*?!

I scream at him and he stays silent for a moment. "You didn't know?" Now this shocks me.

My muscles turn slack. "You- You what?" It's my turn to sound dull and almost unresponsive with a white-r face. My stomach rolls.

There's pounding on the apparently locked back door of the library, cameras and arms flailing and flashing from the little glass window.

  "How could you not know?" He chuckles. I flush. "You didn't tell me..." I whisper.

  "I'm everywhere, honey-" My heart flutters, receding from the banging for a beat.

  "I just didn't want to sound more stuck up than you already thought I was."

"Constantly waving around 'Hey I'm the president!' is not exactly a pleasant date."

  He goes on. I choke on my breathing. "Oh *god*..." "All this time... I haven't..."

"I haven't been checking my media." "Or looking at signs?"

"Or looking at signs." I admit.
"I mostly just sobbed at home." "Oh honey…" He sets a hand on my thigh, sitting beside me.

This time we're in each other's places. For a second, I picture *him* as the blubbering mess. His touch makes my skin heat up, every hair on my neck and arms standing up like static.

"W-What about the guy you were seen with?" "Aren't you *gay*?!"

"Aundrea, look at me."

I look up. "That man is Joshuah Gray, my cousin." I stare at him duly. "W-Well, one last thing."

He waits patiently, deeply blue eyes boring into me. "What were you reading?"

His cheeks turn pink and he glances at the grass, suddenly interested in the tiny flowers coating the ground.

"A book on flirting with women." I almost laugh, an awkward singular squeal comes out instead and everything hits me.

Oh.

I'm the jerk.

"I didn't know..." I whisper. "I'm sorry I thought you did... Well, except the book..." He whispers back, softly.

Suddenly, my lips are finally pressed against his. How could I ever have held myself back from this?

Our mouths are moving in sink and he gives me access when my teeth ask him for more.

We explore each other's mouths, longing, touching and groping through clothes. He grabs my butt and I'm not offended and I straddle his hips.

"I love you," He grunts, quietly. I suck on his lip, making it mine. They should be. He's mine, willing and... I'm willing.

"I think I'm ready to be vulnerable to you." I whisper back, kissing his neck.

All we did was make out like teenagers but people are looking at us as if we had full on dirty sex out there.

We're disheveled as if we might as well have. We're grinning against the flashes and squeals, clicking and laughter.

Our clothes are untucked and smudged; his neck covered in a variety of colorful marks that I am proud of.

Our hair is messy and tangled, stuck to our foreheads and we're both glowing red.

There we are, grinning like idiots on so many Instagram posts, the front of newspapers and we don't even care.

I've never been one to enjoy being on camera or the front page for that matter but if I get to have this sexy hunk in exchange, I'll take the scandals and photos any day.

I place a kiss to my sleeping 'supposed boyfriends' throat. He stirs and grunts, wrapping an arm around my waist.

We're sitting on a peach couch in a wide room, being interviewed. He's in his signature hot guy big business blue suit but his barely gelled hair is a mess and he's snoring live.

I smile awkwardly, giving him another peck. He mumbles something and I blush. The people around us stare expectantly.

He mumbles something else when I do it again. I feel his hand grip my ass and then he says a little too loudly-

 "If you keep that up, I'll—-------" REDACTED! HAH– People's cheeks are flushed a lot similar to mine with eyes wide.

"FRANK!"

 I shout and he sits up. "Honey– Oh," "Hello, uh that wasn't I uhm..." His face is now red too.

I can't believe we're sitting at our bench, the tree's bright and the sun is shining. Nothing could go wrong.

People try to pester us but we've both gotten used to the public. I smile, staring into his beautiful blue eyes.

He's speaking and people are gasping. "Will you *Marry me*?" My heart stops. Arthur. Arthur no!

"No!"

 I shout and I'm running, in heels, my pastel pink and blue cloudy sundress billowing around my all too bare legs. I feel too vulnerable. It's too much.

I'm hyperventilating into my pillow and sobbing on the couch; my hands are shaking. Why? Why did he ask me that?

That one question is forbidden. We had a nice thing going and he had to ruin it.

"Aw, she looks so beautiful!"

My mother wipes her eyes with a white handkerchief.

I give a small smile to my parents, standing up there in front of everyone.

So many people to disappoint. I look over at my husband, Arthur.

He looks dashing I'll admit in the striking white suit and baby blue tie, his slightly grayed hair slick back in curls over his head.

How did I get here?

Why am I here?

 I do my best not to start crying, holding back the cracked well as he grins at me and waves.

We don't recite vowels and the man to wed us forever continues.

I rub my stomach again, peaking over at the brightly lit pink and white tables, bows on every chair and poll.

 Oh god.

"Do you Aundrea Bloomington take this man to be y-"

My brain comes to a screeching stop as I scream.

"No!"

 I feel pain on my cheek. Arthur slapped me, Hard I know there's a red mark and everyone saw but I don't care.

I'm not thinking, barreling back down the aisle. My wedding dress is dirty and ripped and I've gone and lost my shoes but at least I'm far away from him.

I sit down on the damp grass and hug my shoulders, sobbing as it begins to gently rain. Oh great.

The morning after I rip off the sleeves of my gown, beginning my hike.

After a few starving hours I find myself in a library where I meet a woman.

She tells me she'll pay my rent until I get a job. She owns the complex down the street. I nod and sob into her chest.

Two days go by. It's all I need.

I fixed myself a breakfast that was not as incredible as my boyfriend's eggs and discarded them. I made a batch of horrible black coffee that reminded me of our coffee-shop date.

 Of course, I cried into my sofa and didn't drink that either. There's a knock and I go still, somehow knowing it's him. "Frank." I whisper.

"Aundrea."

He quietly nods and I let him in. He didn't bring a raging mob. I settle on the couch. "Coffee?" His face is pale, under his eyes are red.
Did he cry? *Can* he cry?

"What happened?" He guides me to sit behind him and I can't look at him. He doesn't pester. I take a deep breath.

"I've been married before."

He stays silent, setting a hand on my knee. I hold back the whale in my throat. "*Almost* married."

"His name was Arthur Green." I pause and hear him let out a breath.

"He was the picture of manly and handsome, he was a vet with dark brown curls that framed his face and jaw-dropping gorgeous green eyes."

"He hurt me bad." I shudder. His firm grip on my knee tightens but it doesn't hurt. "Really bad, so much so that he made me like this..."

"I left him at the altar." I let my own guilt nip at me as he stays completely silent. "Now don't go on thinking I'm a monster for that..."

I whisper, chewing my tongue. "Go on, you must have had your reasons." I take another breath, willing the clog to let up. It doesn't.

"He did things that I didn't really want and he hurt me when I didn't listen." His grip tightens again. He's angry *with* me.

Not *at me*. "Really bad, Frank and when he found out I was pregnant..."

"My abortion was my biggest regret..." He strokes my leg with his thumb and waits for me patiently, giving me much needed time.

"When I stood there. In front of everyone I knew and loved I just-... I couldn't do it Frank, it felt like a lie."

 He doesn't respond.

 "All online would tell me, was that it was okay and I tried to believe that murdering that innocent child, *my* child was okay but my god Frank I couldn't and it just-... It all hit me on my wedding day."

 "I couldn't say I do and he- He hit me and it burned!"

 I gulped. "It was just one smack too many." I felt my cheek, a ghost ache where he had slapped me.

"I fled and that's when I found that library you brought coffee into."

"For a while I was fine, I'd bury my head in a book, rarely go out and all the more I indulged in media the better, I guess, I felt about myself.

Everyone telling me what I did was right. I did start to believe in it." I paused again.

He just stayed silent, striking my leg comfortingly. "If the media was right about...one thing, then what else were they right about?"

I wiped my eyes and took another throaty breath. This was hard but I'd do it for *him*. I'd be vulnerable and honest with *him*.

For him.

"I stopped wearing dresses and I stopped wearing my hair down." "I stopped talking to other men, especially the white ones."

"The media told me they were evil and I let myself believe because I had met so many that were." "It's not *just* men."

"I stopped talking to people, disconnected except my landlord/librarian. I finally looked up. His face is less pale but that crease between his bushy black brawls is more visible than ever.

He took me in his arms and I pressed myself against his chest, sobbing but continuing because he needed to know if he truly...would eventually marry me.

"But...when I met you," I began in a whisper.

"You scared me because you were everything I was supposed to hate."

"Cocky, senseless and rude and white and of course you were a big wolf-like guy with a wolf-like smile."

"*Wolf-like?*"

I grin, sheepishly.

"When you complimented me, it freaked me out because I actually liked it and how could I possibly like something I wasn't supposed to?"

"The media told me I was brainwashed." I sniff, squeezing the fabric of his suit in my hands. "You were flirting with me, I liked it."

"You liked my sundress so I wore more of them...I-I bought a whole closet full to impress you." "Dress to impress."

He sighed against my hair. I nodded. "When that man attacked me in the women's bathroom, I didn't run out the door or grab my purse...I grabbed you and I held you and- You made me feel..."

I take another deep breath.

"Safe." He kisses my head. "Your car was safe, your house was safe and you- You were safe, ARE safe."

I listened to his soft heartbeat, inhaling his scent. "It terrified me to feel so safe with a man who was so scary." He hummed quietly. Rubbing my scalp with the tip of his nose. It was oddly comforting.

"When you took me to that waterpark, I felt safe and even in the restaurant I felt safe but I think I fell head over heels no turning back in love with you when I woke up on your couch, untouched and you poured us cherry-seven-up in wine glasses and we drank from swirly straws and ate spicy popcorn."

"I knew I was gone by then but I denied it."

"Then you were honest- honest with me and I lost it." "Fell so hard I was afraid you wouldn't catch me and I would slam into the ground but you caught me."

He nods, giving my head more kisses.

"I know with marriage you expect children and a happy wife but I won't always be happy."

I whimpered, afraid that his scent would leave and he would walk out my door, never to see me again but he stayed, yet again.

"You're right, I do expect kids."

He grunted softly. My heart plummeted and the images of the waterpark date and the kids I dreamed of with their pretty blue eyes and black and blonde hair came to light.

Then I remembered the cold doctor smiling at me and reassuring me that an abortion was a fine thing.

I mourned the death of my first almost-borne inside and out.

"But I can wait for you."

He whispered and I stiffened, surprised. "I won't be a happy wife all the time and I can't promise that I'll be a good mom and I have problems!"

He still didn't go.

Why didn't he go?

Why didn't he go!

He just held me in his arms. "I know, Aundrea I know and I love you so I don't care." "I'll try to make you as happy as I can and I can't promise that I'll always be there or that I won't scare you but I sure as hell will try not to."

"I'll try my very hardest." At that moment I knew that he was mine and I was his. That I was safe and it was okay to have a stereotypical romance.

Chapter twenty-five: The stereotypical ending we've all been waiting for

Eventually when I was ready, I proposed and he immediately said yes and picked me up, spinning me around.

We had a litter of three beautiful and growing children. Two boys and one girl. They all had his eyes. The boys had his hair. Charlie, Chris and Lilly.

We moved into a more stable house and we occasionally visit the library.

Life is tough being married to the president where prettier women snatch him away constantly and everyone demands attention but I know he only has eyes and heart for the four of us.

The wedding was beautiful by the way with lots of people trying to barge in but we tried to keep it small.

 Only thing was I refused to wear a wedding gown. I wore my sundress and he wore his suit.

THE END.

Hello,

there

I

hope

you

have

a

lovely

day.

Be safe

Please.

Getting There by Dove Daniels: Teaser

"I promise to have and to hold you forever, I will always love you when your hair isn't pink anymore and when your tits sag, I promise to love you, Shannon."

He spoke heart-felt words in a joking tone, grinning. I smile through tears, wiping my eyes and smearing my mascara. I rub the black ink off onto my sash and kiss him.

That was _six years ago._

The breakupz dozen and nature walks.

My husband of six years just left me. Lost the magic he said, your boobs sag, he says your hair-dye is faded and it reminds me of hay, he says.

Well great. Fine! And on top of that I'm losing interest in my job. Johnny Lee won't take a hint. So, what do I do? I call Nathan my best friend who I always go to when I have a break up.

Except the nice bod guy, I expected to see is not all that pleasant. His belly is bulged, he has another chin and he's just a mess.

Turns out not calling or texting after randomly deciding to hop on a plane with my newlywed wasn't exactly all that kind and Nathan really took it to his big caring heart.

It's up to me now even in *my* life crisis to fix *his* but maybe this is exactly what I need.

***Please support, Willow's Public Library**
@Willowspubliclibarary.com*

Willow public library has been a wonderful place to me. It has been nothing but helpful. I may only go one day a week. (I *hope* to change that.) When I do it's amazing. I can meet people and the staff are really sweet.

Willows public library supplies me with the fuel I need to be able to write. Wonderful guys and gals. Wonderful books.

There're all sorts of genres there. I often come there will a twelve-page list of books and authors they don't have. Instead of kicking me out, or being rude they simply listen, smile, and try their best.

It's a quiet and quaint place with comfortable chairs and even better literature.

This book is not sponsored. I am within my own gratefulness and appreciation to shout out this sweet little library.

  I check out piles and piles each time I go and am never not satisfied. I have never had a bad Willows public library experience.

_I am_ working on a lot plus a series currently and _am_ going to keep writing.